NAME

_____

_____

_____

NOTE

_____

_____

_____

_____

TABLE OF CONTENTS

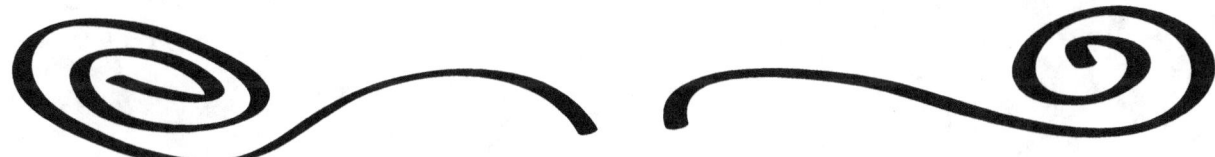

SECTION 1
Angle Lines

SECTION 2
Straight Lines

SECTION 3
Grid Lines

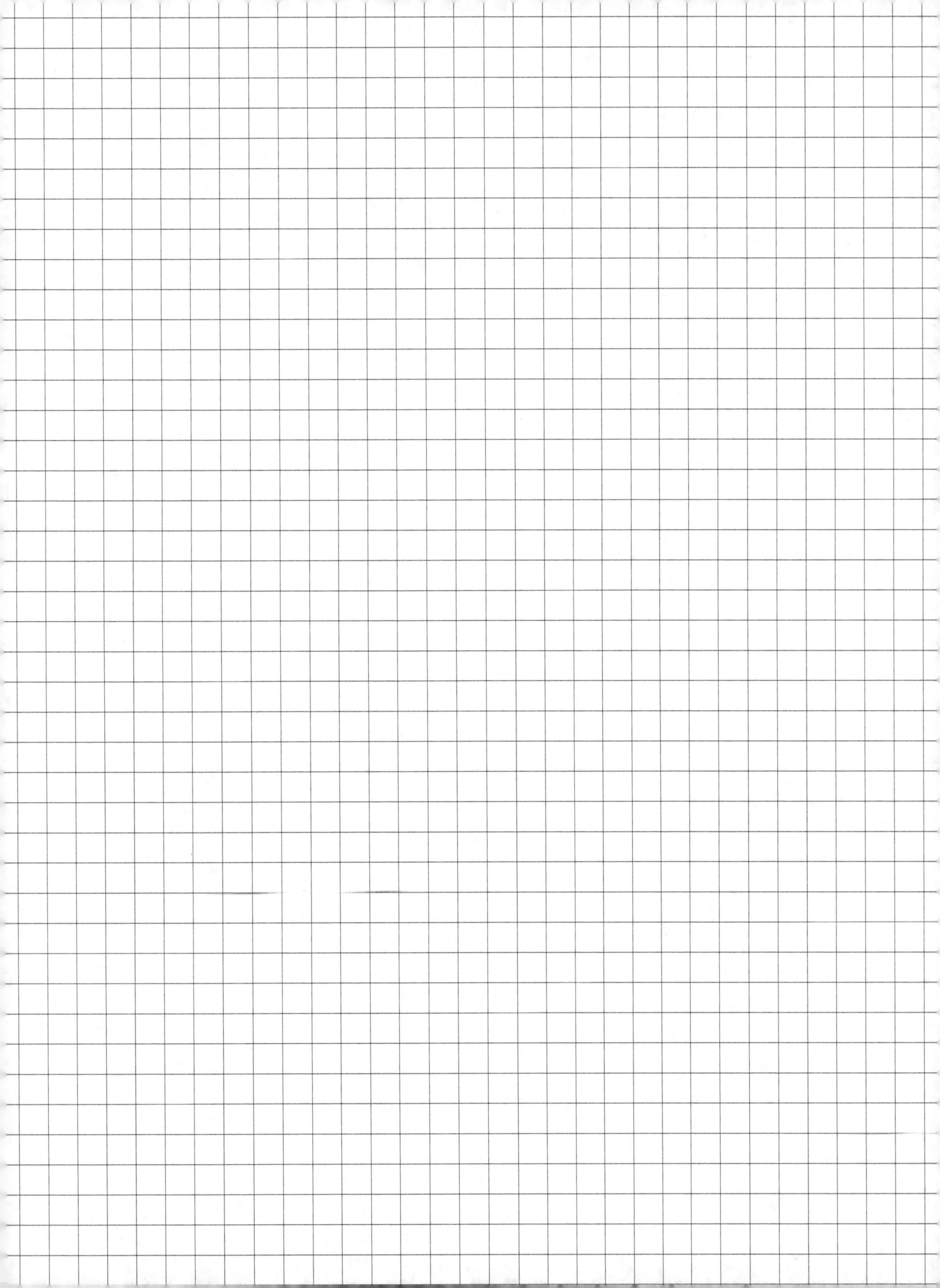

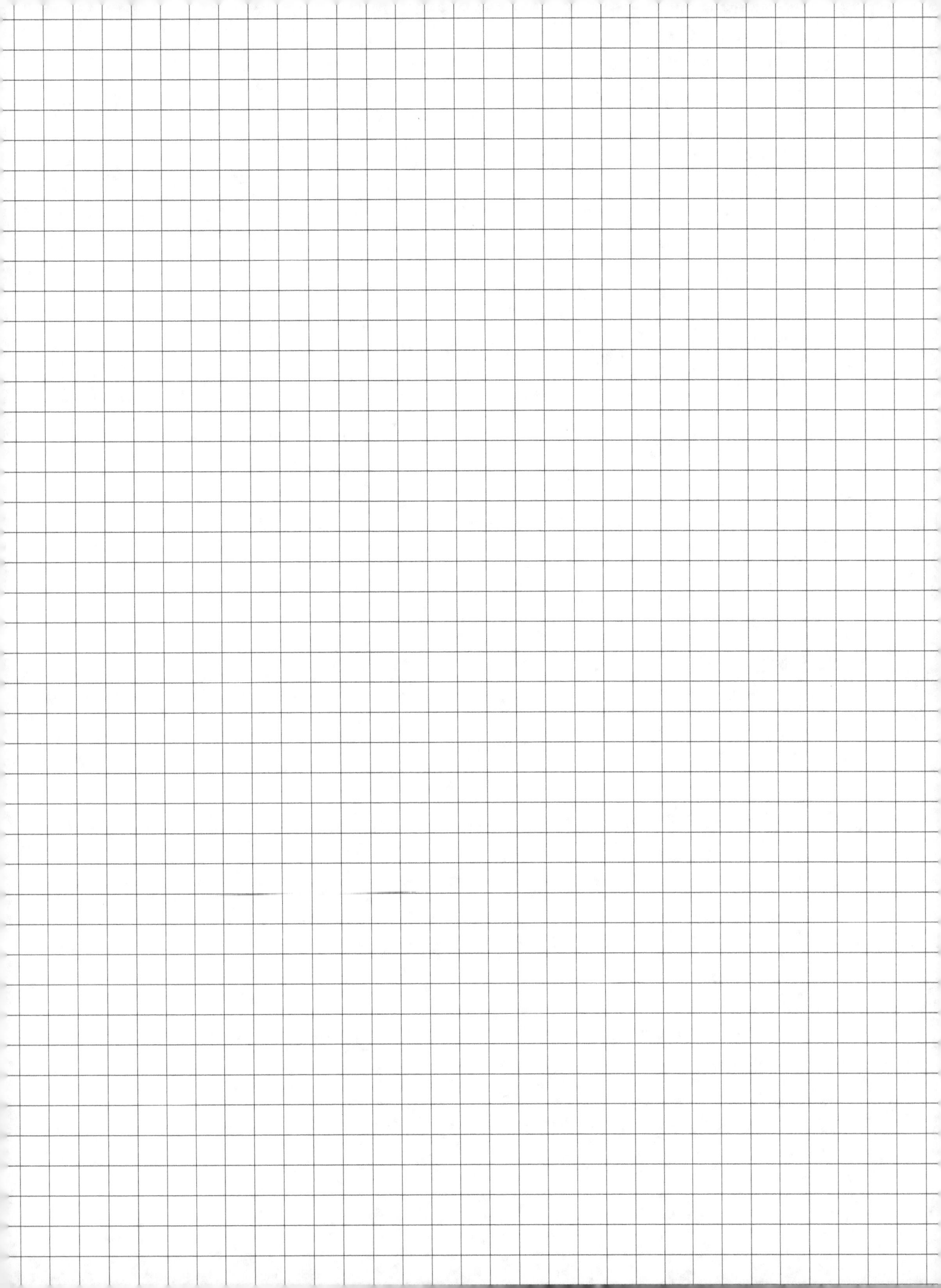

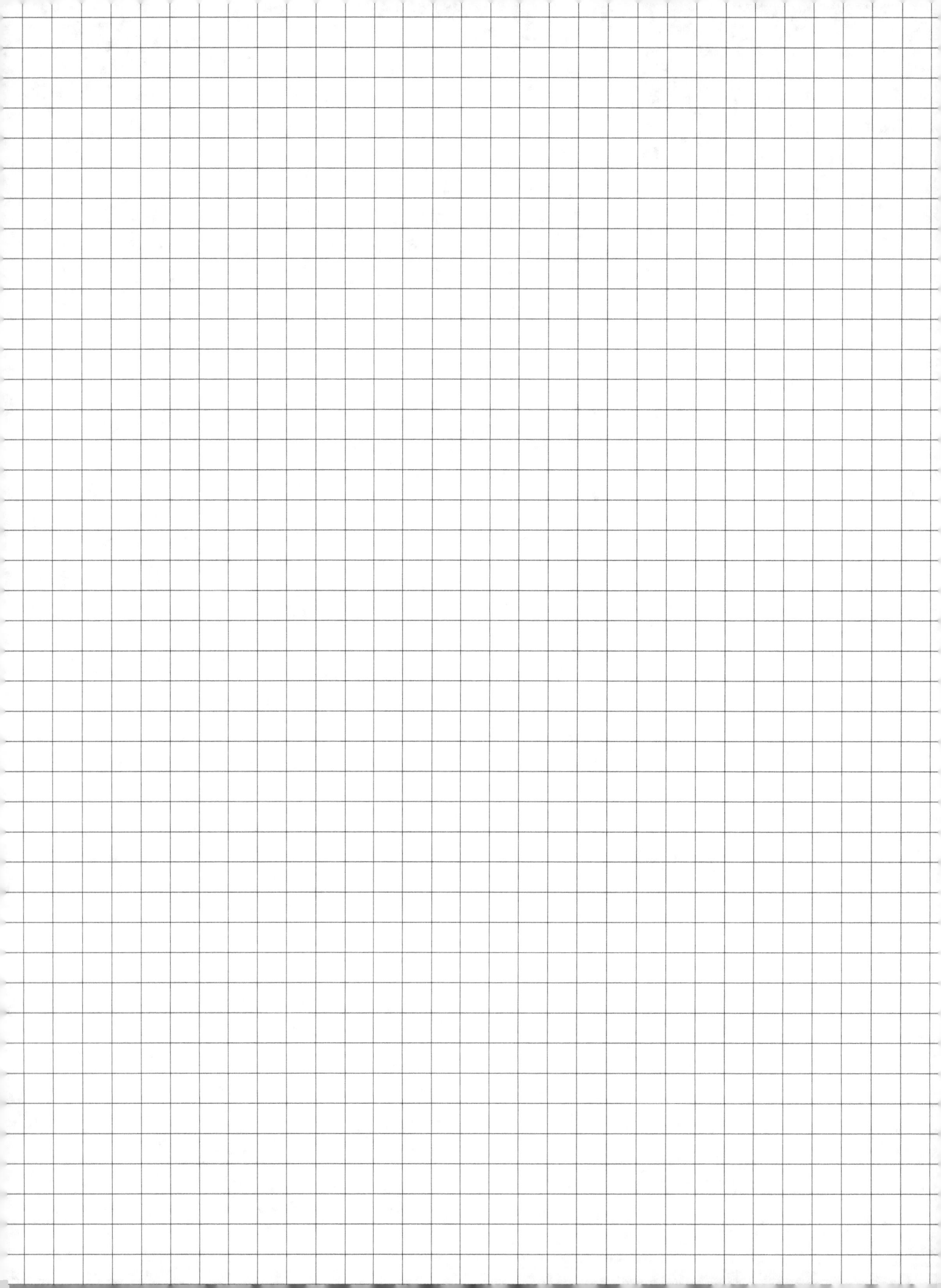

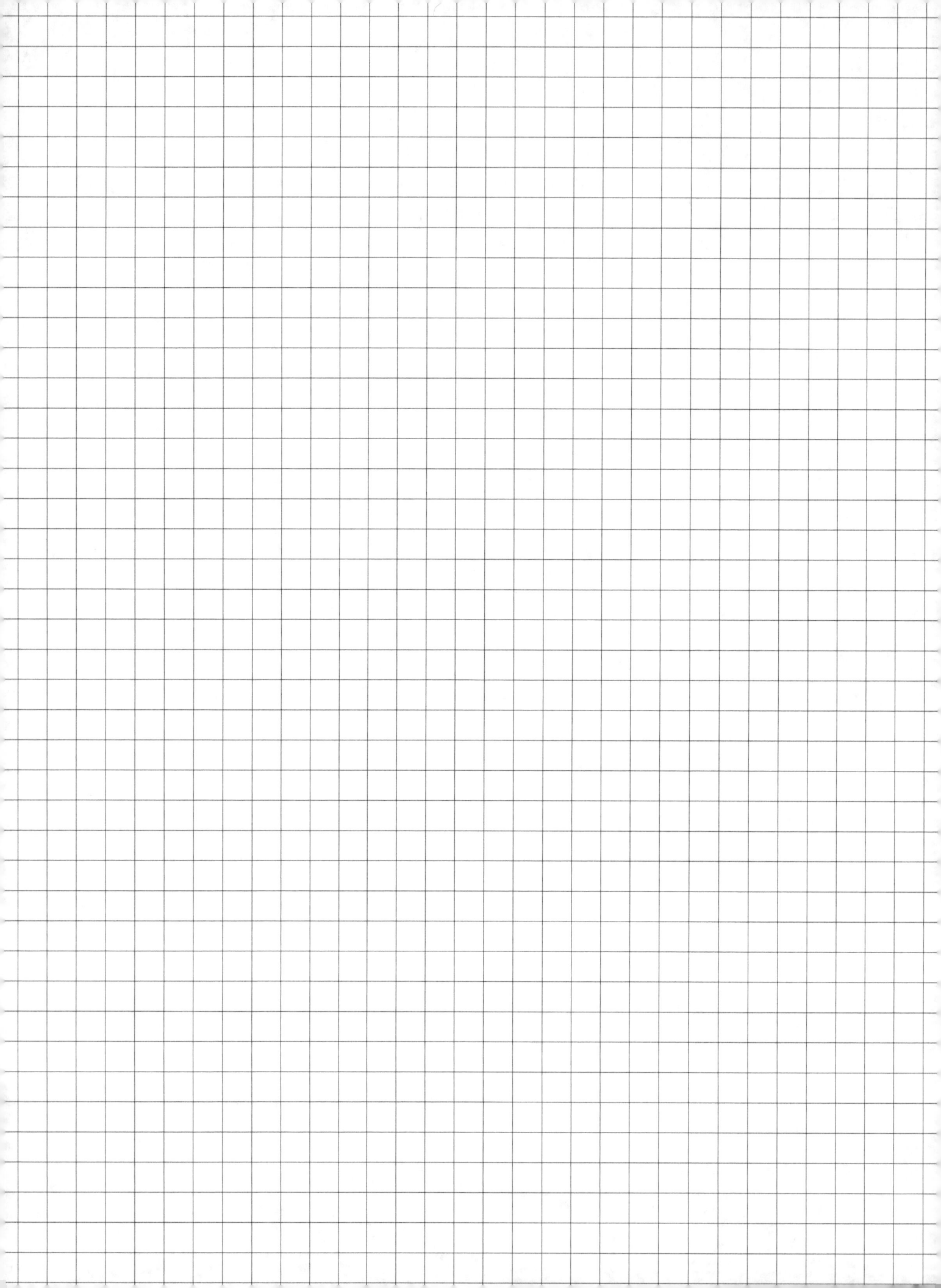

www.ingramcontent.com/pod-product-compliance
Lightning Source LLC
Chambersburg PA
CBHW081302170526
45165CB00011B/3375